A PRE-RAPHAELITE COLLECTION

D. G. ROSSETTI

FORD MADOX BROWN

HOLMAN HUNT

BURNE-JONES

ALBERT MOORE

SIMEON SOLOMON

INCHBOLD

ETC. ETC.

THE GOUPIL GALLERY
LONDON, S.W.

_** *The majority of the Pictures are for sale, and Prices may be had on application.*

NOTE.

A S the collection of pictures formed by the late Mr. Leathart
is more particularly remarkable on the ground of being in
a large measure representative of the so-called pre-Raphaelite
school, it may be as well to say here a few words regarding that
school and the pre-Raphaelite Brotherhood—*quorum pars parva
fui.*

In 1847 and 1848 two students of the Royal Academy—William
Holman Hunt and Dante Gabriel Rossetti, the former in the
painting school, the latter in the antique school—evinced a certain
amount of interest in those developments of art which had pre-
ceded the *cinquecento* and the maturity of Raphael ; some of
their fellow-students applied in derision the term " pre-Raphaelite" to those youths, who, in May, 1848, were aged respectively
twenty-one and twenty.   Mr. Hunt had by that date exhibited a
couple of able paintings—Dante Rossetti none.   There was
another Academy-student, the present Sir John Everett Millais,
P.R.A., then aged nineteen, who had already made a certain
reputation as a painter.   Towards September, 1848, he had in
his hands the engravings by Lasinio, from the old paintings in

the Campo Santo of Pisa. The three young men scanned these engravings with avidity, and they found, and had the boldness to avow to one another, that they were much more in sympathy with that range of art than with the Italian schools which had succeeded Raphael, or with other late developments of European art. Such was the immediate, and in itself rather slight, foundation on which the pre-Raphaelite Brotherhood was based.

Immediately afterwards, four other " Brothers " were enrolled : Thomas Woolner, sculptor ; James Collinson, painter ; Frederic George Stephens, student of painting ; and myself, by vocation a government-clerk, and soon afterwards an art-critic as well. These also were all young men—the oldest being Collinson, who in September, 1848, was twenty-three years of age. No other P.R.B. was ever regularly elected, though Walter Howell Deverell, a painter, was semi-elected after a secession on the part of Collinson, and Bernhard Smith, a sculptor, was viewed with some favour, cut short by his emigrating to Australia.

Of the painters mentioned above, Hunt, Rossetti, and Deverell are represented in Mr. Leathart's collection. Various other painters similarly represented bear a certain close relation to the pre-Raphaelite movement, without being members of the Brotherhood—more especially Madox-Brown, Hughes, Martineau, Inchbold, and Burne-Jones. I name them in their order of date as exhibiting artists.

It has been often said that Madox-Brown was the precursor, or, indeed, the real originator, of the movement ; he has sometimes been called " the grandfather of pre-Raphaelitism " (but he did not relish this term). It is undoubtedly true that before the foundation of the Brotherhood he had exhibited two or three works embodying much the same sort of personal self-expression, and disregard of accepted conventions and commonplaces, which the Brotherhood aimed at. He was also, from the spring of 1848, related to Rossetti as an instructor and guide in the processes of painting, and was soon after well known to Hunt—to Millais, at that early date, barely or not at all. I think it true, therefore, that he "leavened the lump" of pre-Raphaelitism ; but not that he had anticipated it in any such degree as to bereave Hunt, Millais, and Rossetti, of the credit of initiating the movement. In fact, in the course of a year or two, his executive methods became more modified by theirs than theirs had at first been by his. Hughes was a youthful painter greatly in sympathy with the movement, and so was Inchbold ; Martineau studied under the immediate eye of Holman Hunt. Burne-Jones, an Oxford undergraduate, destined for the church, but gifted with high powers of romantic design, sought out Rossetti towards June, 1856, and showed him some drawings. Rossetti told him at once that he ought to be, and must be, an artist, and he became one ; and there are many persons who consider that in Burne-Jones the pre-Raphaelite idea has reached its fullest, highest, and most fascinating expression.

As to the three original members of the pre-Raphaelite Brotherhood there have been two very prevalent misapprehensions—1, that they were prompted by the writings of Ruskin, and 2, that they championed certain speculative or religious ideas. They were, in fact, painters influenced by pictorial ideas. Each of the three was conscious of some high artistic faculty ; and each determined to develop his faculty in accordance to the bent of his own genius, untrammelled by cut-and-dry rules, or by obsolescent or threadbare traditions. They felt that the only way for self-development was to study nature as hard and as closely as they could, but the object of a minute rendering of nature was ultimately to get their own perceptions into a true relation to fact, and so to subserve their own ideas in Art. They perceived that all the great original artists had done the like, while the conventionalists or imitators tried to use the methods of some predecessor as stilts for themselves. They called themselves pre-Raphaelites as signifying, not that they would assimilate to artists preceding Raphael, but that they would discard mannerisms and pomposities, of whatever kind, which had succeeded Raphael.

W. M. ROSSETTI.

THE MERCIFUL KNIGHT. BY SIR EDWARD BURNE JONES, BART.

CATALOGUE.

FORD MADOX BROWN.

1. OURE LADYE OF GOOD CHILDREN.

WATER-COLOUR.   30 by 23 in
Signed " F. Madox Brown, 1847-61."

WILLIAM DAVIS (OF LIVERPOOL).

2. THE SHRIMPER.

OIL.   13½ by 17 in.

On Back :—
" An effect of mist, on the river Mersey. W. Davis, 1855."

ALBERT MOORE.

3. BATTLEDORE.

Oil.

Fan signature.

52 by 17½ in.

See Illustration.

————

WILLIAM DAVIS (of Liverpool).

4. STUBBLE FIELD.

Oil.

Signed "W. Davis."

9 by 13 in.

————

ALBERT MOORE.

5. THE MUSICIAN.

Oil.

Fan signature.

11 by 14¾ in.

BATTLEDORE. BY ALBERT MOORE

(9)

SIMEON SOLOMON.

6. JUDITH GOING TO THE ASSYRIAN CAMP.

WATER-COLOUR.   19½ by 15½ in.

Signed in Monogram, 12-63.

ALBERT MOORE.

7. SHUTTLECOCK.

OIL.   52 by 17½ in.

Fan signature.

LORD LEIGHTON, P.R.A.

8. KING DAVID.

OIL.   37 by 47½ in.

"Oh, that I had wings like a dove; for then would I fly away, and be at rest."

See Illustration.

WM. HOLMAN HUNT.

9. THE DEAD SEA FROM SILOAM.

WATER-COLOUR.   9¼ by 13¾ in.

SIMEON SOLOMON.

10. SAPPHO AND ERINNA.

WATER-COLOUR.   12¾ by 14½ in.

Signed ≶ ≶ 2-64.

" In a garden of Mytilene."

SIR EDWARD BURNE-JONES.

11. THE MERCIFUL KNIGHT.

WATER-COLOUR.   39½ by 27¼ in.

Signed " Edward Burne-Jones, 1863."

On Frame :—

"Of a Knight who forgave his enemy when he might have
destroyed him, and how the image of Christ kissed him in
token that his acts had pleased God."

See Illustration.

King David   By Lord Leighton, P.R.A.

P. F. POOLE, R.A.

12. THE PRODIGAL SON.

Oil.   49 by 36 in.

Signed " P. F. Poole, 1869."

" How many hired servants of my father's have bread
enough and to spare, and I perish here with hunger ! "

Luke xv.

DANTE GABRIEL ROSSETTI.

13. PAOLO AND FRANCESCA.

Water-Colour.   In three compartments.   13 by 24 in.

Francesca, daughter of Guido da Polenta, lord of Ravenna,
was married to Lanciotto, son of Malatesta da Rimini ; she,
however, fell in love with her husband's brother, Paolo, and
the lovers being discovered by Lanciotto, he put them both
to death.

In the first compartment is represented the scene in which
Paolo and Francesca exchange the embrace which is to end
in death, as described in the " Purgatorio,". canto V.   In the
other, the lovers are seen in a close embrace in hell.   While
in the centre, Dante and his guide through hell, Virgil, are
passing them with pitying gaze ; over the two poets' heads
is the inscription, " O Lasso," and below the lovers,
" Quanti dolci pensier, quanto disio menò costoro al doloroso
passo."

Signed D. G. R. (in Monogram), and dated 1862.

When I made answer, I began : " Alas !
How many sweet thoughts and how much desire
Led these two onward to the dolorous pass ! "
Then turned to them, as who would fain inquire,
And said : " Francesca, these thine agonies
Wring tears for pity and grief which they inspire :
But tell me, in the season of sweet sighs,
When and what way did love instruct you so
That he in your vague longings made you wise ? "
Then she to me : " There is no greater woe
Than the remembrance of past happy days
In misery ; and this thy guide doth know.
But if the first beginnings to retrace
Of our sad love, may yield thee solace here,
So will I be as one that weeps and says :

" One day we read, for pastime and sweet cheer,
Of Lancelot, how he found Love tyrannous :
We were alone and without any fear.
Our eyes were drawn together reading thus
Full oft, and still our cheeks would pale and glow ;
But one sole point it was that conquered us.
For when we read of that great lover, how
He kissed the smile which he had longed to win—
Then he whom nought can sever from me now
For ever, kissed my mouth, all quivering.
A pander was the book and he that writ :
Upon that day we read no more therein."
DANTE : *Div. Com., Inf.* c. V.

See Illustration.

PAOLO AND FRANCESCA. BY DANTE GABRIEL ROSSETTI.

ALBERT GOODWIN.

4. SALISBURY.

WATER-COLOUR. 6¼ by 10 in.
Monogram, 1864.

———

DANTE GABRIEL ROSSETTI.

5. BURD-ALANE.

OIL. 1861. 11½ by 12 in.
Signed D. G. R. (in Monogram).

———

DANTE GABRIEL ROSSETTI.

6. THE BOWER GARDEN.

WATER-COLOUR. 13½ by 10 in.
Signed D. G. R. (in Monogram), and dated 1859.

FORD MADOX BROWN.

17. THE ENTOMBMENT OF CHRIST.

WATER-COLOUR.   22½ by 23½ in.

Signed with Monogram, 1869.

On Frame :—

"Then took they the body of Jesus and wrapped it in linen, and laid it in a sepulchre wherein never man before was laid."

———

W. H. DEVERELL.

18. LADY WITH BIRDCAGE.

OIL.   35 by 22 in.

Signed "W. H. △."

———

FORD MADOX BROWN.

19. CHRIST WASHES PETER'S FEET.

WATER-COLOUR.   15½ by 17½ in.

Signed "F. Madox Brown, 1858."

On Frame :—

"After that He poured water into a bason and began to wash the disciples' feet, and to wipe them with the towel wherewith he was girded."—*John* xiii. 5.

FORD MADOX BROWN.

20. "THE PRETTY BAA-LAMBS";
OR, SUMMER HEAT.

OIL.   23½ by 29½ in.

Signed "F. Madox Brown, 1851-9."

WILLIAM DAVIS (OF LIVERPOOL).

21. THE THAMES, NEAR RICHMOND.

OIL.   11½ by 17½ in.

G. SHALDERS.

22. LANDSCAPE.

WATER-COLOUR.   9 by 13 in.

SIMEON SOLOMON.

23. QUEEN ESTHER HEARS OF HAMAN'S PLOT
FOR THE DESTRUCTION OF HER PEOPLE.

DRAWING IN SEPIA.   11½ by 14 in.

1860.

Esther iii. & iv.

SIMEON SOLOMON.

24. BY THE WATERS OF BABYLON.

> " By the waters of Babylon we sat down and wept : when we remember thee, O Sion.
>
> " As for our harps we hanged them up upon the trees that are therein. For they that led us away captive required of us   song, and melody in our heaviness :
>
> " ' Sing us one of the songs of Sion.'   How shall we sing the Lord's song in a strange land ? "
>
> *Psalm cxxxvii.*

DRAWING.   8½ by 13½ in.

SIMEON SOLOMON.

25. ST. MICHAEL OF GOOD CHILDREN.

WATER-COLOUR.   11½ by 8 in.

Signed in Monogram 5-64.

On Back :—

"Dedicated to the memory of William Blake."

WILLIAM DAVIS (OF LIVERPOOL).

26. MOWING.

OIL.   10 by 12 in.

On Back :—

" William Davies, of Liverpool, June, 1860."

WM. HOLMAN HUNT.

27. THE HIRELING SHEPHERD.

OIL.   29 by 52 in.

Signed " W. Holman Hunt. Ewell. 1851."

" Sleepest or wakest thou, jolly shepherd ?
Thy sheep be in the corn ;
And for one blast of thy minikin mouth,
Thy sheep shall take no harm."

Mr. Holman Hunt painted this picture in rebuke of the sectarian vanities and vital negligences of the nation. The shepherd, neglecting his sheep, is trifling with a death's-head moth which he has caught. Touched with superstition, he shows it to a siren of the fields, a girl who laughs at him for a fool, while the sheep are jumping a rivulet into the cornfield.

See Illustration.

SIMEON SOLOMON.

28.

" Who is he that cometh from Edom with dyed gar-ments from Bozrah ?"

Isaiah lxiii., 1 *to* 4.

WATER-COLOUR.   11½ by 7 in.

Signed in Monogram, 1862.

W. J. J. C. BOND.

29. CARNARVON CASTLE : EARLY MORNING. 1862.

OIL.   8¼ by 12½ in.

ALBERT GOODWIN.

30. ST. AUBIN'S BAY, JERSEY.

Monogram, 1864.

WATER-COLOUR.　　　　　　　　　　4¼ by 13¾ in.

———

SIMEON SOLOMON.

31. ISAIAH   REPROVING   THE   WOMEN   OF
JERUSALEM.

Isaiah iii., 16-24.

DRAWING IN SEPIA.　　　　　　　　12 by 17 in.

Signed S S.   6-61 to 6-63.

———

THOMAS BARRETT.

32. LANDSCAPE.

WATER-COLOUR.　　　　　　　　　6¼ by 12½ in.

———

FORD MADOX BROWN.

33. THE PRISONER OF CHILLON ENTREATING
HIS JAILERS TO BURY HIS BROTHER
WHERE THE SUN MIGHT FALL UPON
HIS GRAVE.

WATER-COLOUR.　　　　　　　　　5 by 3¾ in.

Signed on back " Ford Madox Brown, 1858."

DAVID SCOTT.

34. THE SPIRIT OF THE LYRE.

OIL. 22 by 18½ in.

ARTHUR HUGHES.

35. GIPSIES.

OIL. 13½ by 18 in., oval.

DANTE GABRIEL ROSSETTI.

36. THE CHRISTMAS CAROL.

WATER-COLOUR. 13 by 11½ in.

Signed D. G. R. (in Monogram), and dated Xmas, 1857-8.

ARTHUR HUGHES.

37. HOME FROM WORK.

OIL. 40½ by 31 in., arched top.

Signed "Arthur Hughes."

WM. BELL SCOTT.

38. AILSA CRAIG AND ARRAN : A SUMMER-DAY BY THE SEA.

OIL.   13 by 18½ in.

Signed " W. B. Scott, July, 1860."

———

FORD MADOX BROWN.

39. KING LEAR.

OIL.   28½ by 39½ in., arched top.

Signed " F. Madox Brown."

On Frame :—

CORDELIA : Had you not been their Father, these white flakes
Had challenged pity of them.   Was this a face
To be exposed against the warring winds ?
To stand against the deep dread-bolted thunder ?
                    Mine enemy's dog,
Though he had bit me, should have stood that night
Against my fire !   And wast thou fain, poor Father,
To hovel thee with swine, and rogues forlorn,
In short and musty straw ?

ARTHUR HUGHES.

40.   "IT IS THE LITTLE RIFT WITHIN THE LUTE
   THAT BY-AND-BY WILL MAKE THE MUSIC MUTE,
      AND EVER WIDENING SLOWLY SILENCE ALL.
   THE LITTLE RIFT WITHIN THE LOVER'S LUTE,
   OR LITTLE-PITTED SPECK IN GARNER'D FRUIT,
      THAT ROTTING INWARD, SLOWLY MOULDERS ALL."

OIL.   21 by 36½ in., arched top.
           Signed " Arthur Hughes."

DANTE GABRIEL ROSSETTI.

41. SIR TRISTRAM AND LA BELLE YSEULT.

WATER-COLOUR.   24 by 22½ in.
        Signed D. G. R. (in Monogram), and dated 1867.

This picture represents an incident in the *Morte d'Arthur*.
Sir Tristram is bringing King Mark's betrothed to Cornwall.
He and La Belle Yseult, draped in rich deep greens and
blues, are standing in the cabin of the ship, while round
them floats the Spirit of Love on crimson wings.   On a chest
with linen cover rests a ewer containing the love drink.   Sir
Tristram raises the fair lady's hand to his lips, and, as their
goblets touch, the charmed potion bursts into flame.

J. W. INCHBOLD.

42. BOLTON ABBEY.

OIL.   19½ by 27 in.
          Signed " J. W. Inchbold, '53."

DANTE GABRIEL ROSSETTI.

43. SALUTATIO BEATRICIS: IN TERRA ET IN EDEN.

OIL.   Each of the two compartments 29½ by 32 in.

Frame decorated by the Artist.

The compartment entitled "Negli occhi porta la mia Donna amore," with the following inscription above: "Questa mirabile Donna apparve a me, vestita di colore bianco, in mezzo di due gentili donne de più lunga etade.

(VITA NUOVA, *cap.* II.),"

represents a piazza in Florence with Dante ascending the stone steps, as Beatrice, between two gentle ladies older than herself, descends.   Dante is overpowered by Beatrice's loveliness, as he receives that memorable salutation, which inspired him with undying love.

The central figure depicts Love extinguishing the torch; the dial points to the ninth hour, the hour of Beatrice's death, with the date of her death—"9 Jun: 1290"—above; and below, "Quomodo sedet sola civitas!" the first words of that lamentation from Jeremiah which Dante used when, after Beatrice's death, all the city seemed desolate: "How doth the city sit solitary, that was full of people! how is she become a widow, she that was great among nations!"

In the compartment entitled "Guardami ben: ben son, ben son Beatrice," with the following inscription above: "Sovra candido vel cinta d'uliva, Donna m'apparve sotto verde manto Vestita di color di Fiamma viva.

(DIV. COM. *Purg. C.* xxx.),"

Dante is entering the "new spring" of Paradise, while Beata Beatrix, attended by two damsels playing citherns, comes forward to greet him, drawing aside her white veil to assure him that she is indeed Beatrice, and gazing intently into the eyes of her laurelled lover, who returns her gaze in patient silent reverence.

See Illustration.

The Salutation of Beatrice. By Dante Gabriel Rossetti.

SIR EDWARD BURNE-JONES.

44. CLARA VON BORK, 1560.

WATER-COLOUR.   13½ by 7 in.

Signed " E. Jones, pinxit 1860."

SIR EDWARD BURNE-JONES.

45. BUONDELMONTE'S WEDDING. FLORENCE, A.D. 1215.

A DRAWING IN INDIAN INK.   10 by 30 in.

SIR J. NOEL PATON, R.S.A., LL D.

46. NIMROD.

OIL.   13½ by 18 in.

On Back :

"Painted by J. Noel Paton, and by him presented to me. Charles Black."

SIR EDWARD BURNE-JONES.

47. SIDONIA VON BORK, 1560. (THE SORCERESS.)

WATER-COLOUR.   13 by 6½ in.

Signed " 1860.   E. Burne-Jones fecit."

SIR EDWARD BURNE-JONES.

48. MERLIN AND NIMUË.

WATER-COLOUR.   25¼ by 20 in.

Signed "E. B. J., 1861."

On Frame :—

" And always Merlin lay about the Lady, for to have her to himself, and she was ever passing weary of him and fain would have been delivered of him, for she was afraid of him because he was a Devil's son, and she could not put him away by no means.

" And upon a time it happened that Merlin showed to her where was a great wonder wrought by enchantment, which went under a stone.   So by her subtle craft and working, she made Merlin to go under that stone to let her wit of the marvels there.

" But she wrought so for him that he came never out for all the craft that he could do."

Morte d'Arthur, c. 60.

On Back, in the Artist's writing :—

" E. Burne-Jones.

" The enchantment of Nimuë : how by subtilty she caused Merlin to pass under a heaving stone into a grave."

₀ This has been purchased by the authorities of the South Kensington Museum.

WILLIAM THE CONQUEROR FINDING THE BODY OF HAROLD. BY FORD MADOX BROWN.

THOMAS STOTHARD, R.A.

(B. 1755.   D. 1834.)

49. INTEMPERANCE.

> Design of the subject of Intemperance painted on the great staircase at Burleigh, the seat of the Most Honourable the Marquis of Exeter.

O:L.   A.D. MDCCCII.   21 by 29 in.

————

FORD MADOX BROWN.

50. WILLIAM THE CONQUEROR FINDING THE BODY OF HAROLD AFTER THE BATTLE OF HASTINGS.

OIL.   41 by 48 in.

> Signed " F. Madox Brown, 1844 to 1861."

On Frame :—

> Willielmus Conquistator.
> Hic ferunt corpus Haraldi Willelmo Duci.

See Illustration.

J. W. INCHBOLD.

51. THE LAGOON, VENICE.

OIL.

Signed " J. W. Inchbold, Venice." $13\frac{1}{2}$ by $20\frac{1}{2}$ in.

WM. BELL SCOTT.

52. RETURNED FROM THE LONG CRUSADE.

WATER-COLOUR. 23 by $18\frac{1}{2}$ in.

ALFRED W. HUNT.

53. MOUNTAIN LANDSCAPE.

WATER-COLOUR. $9\frac{1}{2}$ by 14 in.

WM. BELL SCOTT.

54. THE VISIT OF BOCCACIO TO DANTE'S DAUGHTER.

WATER-COLOUR. 13 by $17\frac{1}{2}$ in.

R. B. MARTINEAU.

55 KATHARINA AND PETRUCHIO.

The Taming of the Shrew.

OIL.   35 by 28 in.

Signed, with Monogram, 1855.

———

WILLIAM DAVIS (OF LIVERPOOL).

56. FIELD OF GREEN CORN.

OIL.   12 by 15½ in.

Signed "W. Davis."

———

A. LEGROS.

57. NEAR AMIENS.

WATER-COLOUR.   16 by 23½ in.

———

WILLIAM TURNER (OF OXFORD).

58. OXFORD.

WATER-COLOUR.   13 by 22¼ in.

HENRY MOORE, R.A.

59. SEA PIECE.

OIL.   20½ by 39½ in.

Signed " H. Moore, 1867."

———————

WM. ETTY, R.A

60. AN ORIENTAL.

OIL.   10 by 7½ in.

———————

DAVID SCOTT.

61. THE CHALLENGE.

OIL.   55 by 67 in.

———————

OLD MASTER.

62. ITALIAN GENTLEMAN AND SERVANT.

OIL.   48 by 36½ in.

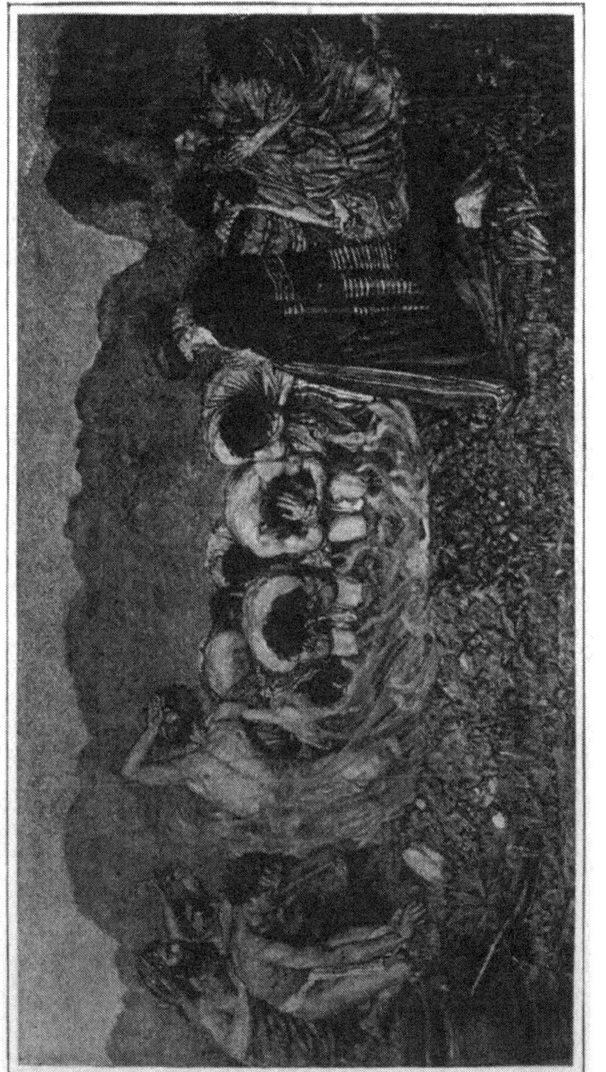

ELIJAH'S SACRIFICE. BY ALBERT MOORE.

ALBERT MOORE.

63. ELIJAH'S SACRIFICE.

OIL.   38½ by 70 in.

> "Then the fire of the Lord fell, and consumed the burnt offering, and the wood, and the stones, and the dust, and licked up the water that was in the trench. And when all the people saw it they fell on their faces : and they said "The LORD, he is God; the LORD, he is God."
>
> *I. Kings, xviii.*

See Illustration.

WM. BELL SCOTT.

64. HEXHAM.

OIL.   20 by 26 in.

WILLIAM DAVIS (OF LIVERPOOL).

65. RYEWATER, NEAR LEIXLIP, CO. KILDARE, IRELAND.

OIL.   20 by 30 in.

On Back :—
"William Davis."

MARK ANTHONY.

66. "NIGHT, STORM, AND DARKNESS."

Oil.   61 by 45½ in.

> Painted in the year 1870, in the Park of Aldermaston near Reading.

A. LEGROS.

67. THE WOODCUTTER.

Oil.   51 by 68½ in.

ALFRED W. HUNT.

68. STREAM IN CARNARVONSHIRE.

Oil.   14 by 19½ in.

WM. BELL SCOTT.

69. THE GLOAMING : MANSE GARDEN IN BERWICK-
SHIRE.

OIL..   15½ by 24 in.

Signed " W. B. Scott, 1863."

———

J. W. EWBANK, R.S.A.

70. SEAPIECE.

OIL.   24 by 36 in.

———

WM. ETTY, R.A.

71. NEGRO BOY.

OIL.   24¼ by 19 in.

WM. BELL SCOTT.

72. "THE KING'S QUAIR."

SCREEN PAINTED IN OILS.

Illustrating the early Scottish poem, written by the first James of Scotland, when a prisoner at Windsor in 1420, on his love for Lady Jane.

Also a selection of Blue China Vases and Jars, an Oriental Plate, Coloured Jars, a Pair of Storks, and others

PRINTED BY J. S. VIRTUE AND CO., 294, CITY ROAD LONDON.

FIGARO-SALON, 1896.

Illustrated by the Typogravure Process.

TEXT IN FRENCH BY PH. GILLE.

Complete in 6 parts at **1s. 8d.** each; index and title-page, **6d.;** cloth case, **2s. 6d.**; bound complete, **14s.**

ÉDITION DE LUXE.

2 sets on Japanese Paper, in-folio, complete **£4**
10 sets on Papier Marais, in-folio, complete **£2**

*** *Volumes since* 1886 *also to be had at similar prices.*

SALON, 1896.

ENGLISH EDITION.

Illustrated with about 100 Plates by the Goupilgravure Process.

Ordinary edition, papier vélin, bound in red cloth **£2 12 6**

SALON, 1896.

Illustrated with about 100 Plates by the Goupilgravure Process.

To commence about May, 1896.

COMPLETE IN TWELVE PARTS, NOT SOLD SEPARATELY.

Price **£2 8s.** complete, with title-page and index; **£2 12s. 6d.,** bound in red cloth.

ÉDITION DE LUXE.

10 sets upon Japanese Paper, with 24 duplicate plates, printed on Japanese Paper, **£6** complete.

BOUSSOD, VALADON & CO.,
Fine Art Publishers to Her Majesty.

QUEEN ELIZABETH.

BY

THE RIGHT REV. MANDELL CREIGHTON, D.D.

Bishop of Peterborough.

AS a fitting pendant to the remarkably successful work on "Mary Stuart," Messrs. BOUSSOD, VALADON & Co. have arranged to publish a volume of the same size, and at least artistic merit, entitled "Queen Elizabeth." The text will be written by the Bishop of Peterborough, whose writings on the period are well known and highly esteemed.

The volume will be illustrated by a fac-simile Portrait in colours as a frontispiece, and by various other portraits of Queen Elizabeth and the notabilities of her reign. These will be reproduced from the originals which have been lent for the purpose by H.M. The Queen, the Marquis of Salisbury, Earl Spencer, Earl Dysart, and others.

There will be two Editions for Great Britain published on the following terms :—

Édition de Luxe, on Japanese paper throughout, each copy numbered, limited to 200 copies for sale, with a few additional copies for presentation (not exceeding 25). Of these nearly all have already been subscribed . . . £8 0 0

Ordinary Edition, also on good paper, but not numbered £2 8 0

BOUSSOD, VALADON & CO.,

Fine Art Publishers to Her Majesty.

5, REGENT STREET, LONDON, S.W.